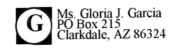

Ms. Gloria J. Garcia
PO Box 215
Clarkdale, AZ 86324

D0889378

At dawn may the Lord bestow
faithful love that I may sing
praise through the night, praise
to the God of my life.
Psalm 42:9

The intent and
purpose of this volume is to
give you faith, hope and
inspiration. Hopefully it will help bring
peace and tranquility into your life. May
it be a reminder of God's love, guidance
and His many blessings.

Our publications help to support our work
for needy children in over 130 countries
around the world. Through our
programs, thousands of children are
fed, clothed, educated, sheltered
and given the opportunity to
live decent lives.

Salesian Missions wishes to extend special thanks and gratitude to our generous poet friends and to the publishers who have given us permission to reprint material included in this book. Every effort has been made to give proper acknowledgments. Any omissions or errors are deeply regretted, and the publisher, upon notification, will be pleased to make the necessary corrections in subsequent editions.

Cover photo: ©Amygdala Imagery/iStockphoto.com

First Edition Printed in the U.S.A. by Concord Litho Group, Concord, NH 03301.

The Dawn of a New Day

from the
Salesian Collection

Compiled and Edited
by Jennifer Grimaldi

Illustrated by
Robert VanSteinburg, Russell Bushée,
Paul Scully, Frank Massa, Dorian Remine,
Jessica Wheeler, Maureen McCarthy,
Bob Pantelone, and Pauline Aikman

Contents

There Is Hope for Tomorrow

There is hope for tomorrow
If you trust God today
For He can remove mountains
That have blocked your way.
There are prayers being answered
Somewhere every day
Because miracles still happen
When we trust and obey.
There is hope for tomorrow
However long the night
For the sun will rise tomorrow
And shed its warming light.

There are things we can't control
That torment or delight,
But faith cannot be explained
In terms of black and white.
There is hope for tomorrow,
It's always been that way,
For sorrows beget blessings
When we believe and pray.
It's always darkest before dawn,
Before the light of day;
There is hope for tomorrow,
It's always been that way!

Clay Harrison

Faith

There is a secret, quiet faith
That sparks the mind and soul.
It believes, in every case,
That God is love alone.
This faith has no expecting
And forms with selfless work.
Our effort is the sacrifice
That fortifies the nerves.
With humility and patience,
Our love and light evolve.
Then every tough decision
Is left for God to solve.

John Frederick Zurn

His Wonder

The earth explodes in majesty
As God presents the scenes,
Of vibrant beauty flourishing
As He nourishes and preens.

The foliage takes changes
As the seasons come and go,
From pink and purple, red and green
To the silver in the snow.

God gives us the golden sun
The blessed rain and morning dew,
He paints the clouds and rainbows
Into our skies of blue.

How wonderful His miracles
So beautifully displayed,
We only need to look about
To see the miracles He's made.

We should search our hearts and thank Him
Giving all our love and praise,
As we see God's wonders here unfold
To brighten all our days.

Patience Allison Hartbauer

*You are my lamp, O Lord! O my God, You
brighten the darkness about me.*
2 Samuel 22:29

O God, restore us and smile on us
so that we may be saved.
Psalm 80:3

This Day

Dawn is breaking... I'm alone
Oh! To face another day,
I must have faith... that God will come
To help me on my way.
I turn to Him with reverence
I seek His guidance in my prayer,
I place my problems... and my fears
In my Savior's loving care.
I trust that God will guide me
In my thoughts and my decisions,
That I will be optimistic
Despite adverse conditions.
For God restores my confidence
As I heed His good advice,
His precious words and promises
Are all I need... they will suffice.
This day I pledge devotion
I shall be exemplary,
Trusting and believing God
Will spend this day with me.

Patience Allison Hartbauer

Let Your love come to me,
Lord, salvation in accord
with Your promise.
Psalm 119:41

A Perfect Day

Walk with me in the morning hours
When the dew's still heavy on the flowers;
When birds awaken from nightly rest
And the sun rises o'er the mountain crest.

Walk with me in the noontide hours
Down country lanes where pine trees tower,
Drinking in joys at the peak of day,
Tasting the beauties that God has made.

Walk with me in the sunset hours,
See the twilight and evening showers;
Then at the end of this perfect day
May we give to God our thanks and praise.

Loise Pinkerton Fritz

O Lord, how manifold are Thy works!
In wisdom hast Thou made them all:
the earth is full of Thy riches.
Psalm 104:24

God the Master and Creator

I am glad that I arose this morn
As early as I did,
For I witnessed night's own darkness
Open up it's famous lid.

To a grand and glorious color
Painted by the hands of time,
God the Master and Creator
Chose these colors so divine.

No one else cannot proclaim it
Like the Master Artist can,
He designs and paints the color
Never made by human hand.

And each thing that He completed
Stands the test of humankind,
For He has His own creation
Mortal soul cannot design.

Katherine Smith Matheney

Ingredients

A handful of daydreams
And a poem is begun;
A measure of moonbeams
Stirs a love song that's sung.

Green buds on an oak tree
Cause brown leaves to fall;
Seeds blossom in gardens
And children "stretch tall"!

Longs Summers bring picnics
And strawberries for pies;
White clouds form an icing
For blueberry skies.

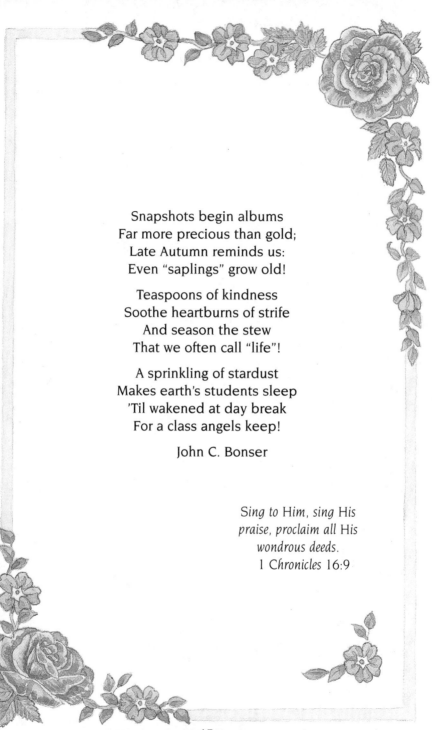

Snapshots begin albums
Far more precious than gold;
Late Autumn reminds us:
Even "saplings" grow old!

Teaspoons of kindness
Soothe heartburns of strife
And season the stew
That we often call "life"!

A sprinkling of stardust
Makes earth's students sleep
'Til wakened at day break
For a class angels keep!

John C. Bonser

Sing to Him, sing His
praise, proclaim all His
wondrous deeds.
1 Chronicles 16:9

Only goodness and love will pursue me all the days of my life; I will dwell in the house of the Lord for years to come.
Psalm 23:6

My Secret Place

There's a secret place within my heart
Where no one else can go.
I enter there when I am sad
Or feeling kind of low.

I dwell upon God's love for me
And the happy times of the past.
I savor and draw strength from them;
The first memory until the last.

Each rhythmic beat of my contented heart
Reminds me that life must go on.
I close the door to my secret place
For now my blues have gone.

Shirley Hile Powell

*I will praise You, Lord, with
all my heart; I will declare all
Your wondrous deeds.*
Psalm 9:2

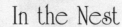

In the Nest

The mother robin feeds her young,
And in the nest they stay,
Eagerly awaiting,
The food she brings today.

For it will help them to be strong,
And someday, try their wings,
She shelters them, and with each morsel,
Love is what she brings.

We're in God's nest, He's feeding us,
Just like the baby birds,
And each day we are stronger,
As we feed upon His word.

Connie J. Kirby

As the sparrow finds a home and the swallow a nest to settle her young, my home is by Your altars, Lord of hosts, my King and my God!
Psalm 84:4

19

Life Brand New

Let not your heart be troubled
Nor laden with despair
For God sent His only Son, Jesus,
And gave us His kingdom to share.
For if we keep His promises
And have faith that His word is true,
He will unfold his mercy
And give us life brand new!

Gloria DeWald

*But you, Lord, my God, deal kindly
with me for Your name's sake; in
Your great mercy rescue me.*
Psalm 109:21

Listen for the Whisper

Listen for the whisper
When you feel there's no one there.
Listen for the whisper
When you are in deep despair.

Listen for the whisper
Through the joy and through the pain.
Listen for the whisper
In that lovely sweet refrain.

Listen for the whisper
In everything you do,
For the Lord is there to help you.
His whisper comes through you.

Ruthmarie Brooks Silver

*If you are willing to listen,
you will learn; if you give
heed, you will be wise.*
Sirach 6:33

Oceanic Symphony

There is music in the ebbing
And the movement of the tide,
How the water rushes to the shore
And shifts the sand aside –
How it softly plants a tender kiss
And saturates the land,
Rejoicing in the velvet touch
Of its Father's loving hand.
There's a cadence that keeps rhythm,
The heartbeat of the sea;
As ocean swell, the metronome,
Ticks on endlessly.

It crescendos with excitement
Or flows to gentle calm,
Repeating its tattoo of joy
From morning 'til next dawn.
An oceanic symphony,
Resplendent in its song;
You can almost hear the violins
As they softly play along –
The gift washed ashore to drift
Along this crippled earth,
To swell across a silent land
In a resurrected birth.
My Father's voice controls the sea
With a measure of pure rhyme –
It scrolls along the depth and shore
To orchestrate its time.
From deep within, a song will rise,
All joined in one accord,
An oceanic symphony
Presented to the Lord.

Nancy Watson Dodrill

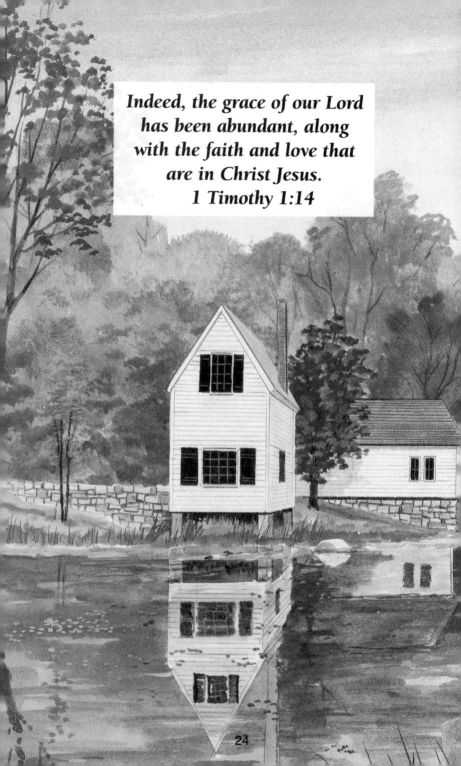

Indeed, the grace of our Lord
has been abundant, along
with the faith and love that
are in Christ Jesus.
1 Timothy 1:14

24

Faith

In youth I caught a glimpse of faith,
As I climbed life's rugged stair,
And filled with awe, I bowed my head,
And breathed a childlike prayer.

Again I saw a loving faith
In a wee child's trusting eyes.
Such wondrous faith in one so small
Quite took me by surprise.

In later years I knew a faith,
So beautiful and strong.
It lead through unfamiliar paths
And cheered my way along.

Again I bowed and gratefully
I thanked a loving God,
For giving me a faith so great
It blessed the path I trod.

Lola E. Dugger

*Whatever you ask for in prayer
with faith, you will receive.*
Matthew 21:22

Let the words of my mouth meet with Your favor, keep the thoughts of my heart before You, Lord, my rock and my redeemer.
Psalm 19:15

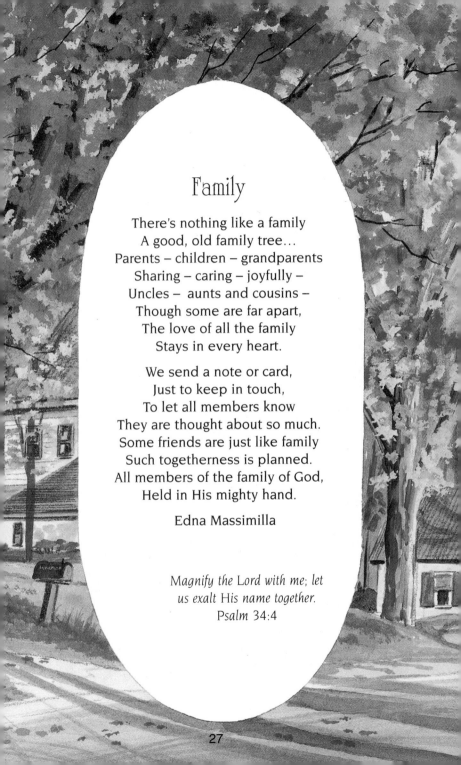

Family

There's nothing like a family
A good, old family tree…
Parents – children – grandparents
Sharing – caring – joyfully –
Uncles – aunts and cousins –
Though some are far apart,
The love of all the family
Stays in every heart.

We send a note or card,
Just to keep in touch,
To let all members know
They are thought about so much.
Some friends are just like family
Such togetherness is planned.
All members of the family of God,
Held in His mighty hand.

Edna Massimilla

*Magnify the Lord with me; let
us exalt His name together.*
Psalm 34:4

Possible Dreams

Many dreams are realized,
Some never to mature.
God knows the dream you're dreaming –
He put it there for sure.
It's possible to reach this goal
To make your dream come true.
Pray and ask for guidance,
He'll do the rest for you.
If you believe – you shall achieve
And victory will be yours,
And the Master who has all the keys
Can open many doors.

Helen Parker

28

My Friend

I talk to my Friend,
Never missing a day.
I know that He listens
In His own special way.

Some days may be sad,
Others, happy and gay,
But I always find comfort
When I quietly pray.

My blessings are many
And given with love,
For my heart knows the giver –
It's my Friend from above.

Erna Gwillim

*May the Lord give might to
His people; may the Lord
bless His people with peace!*
Psalm 29:11

29

Faith

So many things we do not know
As on life's journey we must go.
Like little children in His care,
We trust! And know that He is there.

But oft we do not see His plan,
So dimly lit the mind of man.
Yet stand we must, yes, straight and tall,
To reach His hand held out to all.

Remember God is always near
And cares for us who linger here.
He answers every prayer, you'll see!
His love is great for you and me.

This love He chose to give it birth
For us, His children here on earth,
By giving us His son divine
To die for sins both yours and mine.

Within His passion on the cross
Reflected there our pain and loss.
Yet every sorrow we must bear,
With God's own Son's it can't compare.

Bernice Laux

*I will listen for the word of God;
surely the Lord will proclaim peace
to His people, to the faithful, to
those who trust in Him.*
Psalm 85:9

Greatest Treasures

There are many things God gives for pleasure
That have become my greatest treasure:
The bluest skies, clouds that flow,
A snowflake falling, a sunset's glow.
But He also offers gifts each day –
Precious ones that only I can give away:
Gentle touches, smiles on display,
A friendly visit, kind words to say.
There are many things God gives for pleasure
That have become my greatest treasure.

Barbara Joan Million

Keep Hope in Your Heart

If you have hope in your heart
Then you'll be rich as a king,
For with hope in your heart
You can do anything.
If you have hope in your heart
Your day will happy be,
Then you'll find peace of mind,
Just try and you'll see.
If you have hope in your heart
You'll never feel sad,
And all of your days
Will surely be glad.

Nora M. Bozeman

May Your kindness, Lord,
be upon us; we have put
our hope in You.
Psalm 33:22

33

For wisdom will enter your heart,
knowledge will please your soul,
Proverbs 2:10

God's Paintings

The mornings have grown chilly now,
Fog hugs the windowpane;
The grass is wet with morning dew
Or was it evening rain?
Gold and red leaves have fallen,
Trees stand tall and bare;
On the woven webs of spiders
Wet droplets glisten there.
Soon the winds of Winter
Will howl throughout the land;
Tree branches will seem to shiver
Everywhere they stand.
Soon Winter snow will softly fall
To cover every tree;
White will be the color
Everywhere we see.
Frost will etch the windows
And seal the windowpane,
Then the Winter sun will shine
To melt it all again.
And so the seasons come and go,
The years pass so swiftly by;
God's paintings on our windows
To pleasure you and I.

Milly Patzer

Come and see the works of God,
awesome in the deeds done for us.
Psalm 66:5

A Lesson From a Little Bird

A little bird high on a branch
Does what he can do best.
He sits and sings with all his might
And leaves to God the rest.

He is not anxious about food,
For God himself will give
The little morsels day by day
That give him strength to live.

Should we be worried when we think
About our needs today?
Does God, who made the universe,
Not hear us when we pray?

And lovingly He does provide
As seasons come and go,
Remembering the little birds
That do not reap nor sow.

Regina Wiencek

Every Day

I often sit alone and think
Of wondrous times gone by.
And realize each day I'm given
Is a blessing from on high.

Today is just as dear
As those yesterdays to me.
And some tomorrow, sweeter still;
The day my Lord I'll see.

M. Elaine Fowser

Show them You alone are the Lord,
the Most High over all the earth.
Psalm 83:19

Bless the Families

Bless the families, Lord, I meet
Along life's busy way;
Keep them safe within Your care
And hear them when they pray.
Bless the father who gives strength
When trials are hard to meet;
Bless the mother whose loving touch
Makes the home more sweet.
Bless the little children, Lord,
Watch o'er them at their play;
They are too young to know
Where the hidden dangers lay.

Bless the older children, too,
As they rush off to school;
May they learn at early age
To live the golden rule.
Bless the families everywhere –
This is my humble plea;
Guide them and protect them Lord
Wherever they may be.

Kay Hoffman

Step Out in Faith

Do you face a river too wide to cross,
Is there doubt and fear in your heart?
By faith step into the waters below
And the river before you will part.
God is still God and He doesn't change,
What He once did He will do again.
His promises given never fail,
Forever they stay the same.
So face every river with confidence,
Let faith rise up in your heart.
In the name of the Lord step into the deep
And the waters before you will part.

Regina Wiencek

Special Treasures

There are treasures everywhere –
Across the earth and in the air.
The sun beyond a sky of gray;
The peacefulness of every day.
The joy each time we meet a friend –
A song we hope will never end.
Tiny buds deep in the grass
Soon to bloom in a colored mass;
Shadows on a Winter snow;
Stars at night with constant glow.
There are special treasures everywhere;
Made by God for us to share.

Joan Stephen

*For where your treasure is, there
also will your heart be.*
Matthew 6:21

Life's Roads

Down a winding road I wander,
Walking on, not knowing where.
Not caring much as I ponder,
Still assured that God is there.
I'll go where'er He wants me to
I'll let Him lead the way.
He'll hold my hand and I'll be safe
Throughout each hour of the day.
Life's roads can sometimes seem quite rugged
With stumbling blocks to mar the way,
Yet, as long as He is still near
I know He'll take them all away.

Down the winding roads there's beauty
Greeting me on every side…
O'er hill and dale and fields of snow
Across the mountains far and wide.
Life's roads are wonderful to travel
With my Savior as my guide.
My soul in sweet fulfillment is nourished –
Completely satisfied.

Lou Ella Cullipher

May Others See Thee in Me

Thank You, dear Father, for being there
When I have needed Thee,
And may I ever, always hear
Whenever You're calling me.

To be Your faithful witness, Lord,
To others far and wide –
Telling them of Thy precious love
And concern, what e'er betide.

Give me the strength that I may need
And a heart so filled with care,
That others see Thee – living in me,
And with You all their burdens share.

Mary S. Chevalier

*Therefore, you shall love the
Lord, your God, with all your
heart, and with all your soul,
and with all your strength.*
Deuteromy 6:5

God's Great Love

There are so many ways God shows us His love
By sending His gifts from Heaven above,
The sun and the rain, the flowers and trees,
The moon and the stars, a soft Summer breeze,
A baby's sweet smile and a warm gentle touch,
He shows that He loves us so very much.
When you feel down and alone, and think no one cares
Look to our Lord for the love that He shares,
For when we are sad, He makes our hearts rise
And wipes the tears away from our eyes,
His love is omniscient if we take time to see,
For there's no greater love than God's love for you and me.

Nettie Gornick

How great are Your
works, Lord! How
profound Your purpose!
Psalm 92:6

I'd Like to Share...

I'd like to share my joy with you,
And also share my pain;
I'd like to share a sunny day,
And also one of rain...

I'd like to take you by the hand,
And wander down the road;
I'd like to know when you are sad,
And help to lift your load...

I'd like to spend an afternoon,
And chat with you awhile;
I'd like to hear about your cares,
And see your gentle smile…

I'd like to help you write a verse,
Or sing a happy song;
I'd like to journey to a star,
And have you come along…

There are so very many things,
I'd like to do with you,
So let's join forces, you and I,
And see what we can do!

Hope C. Oberhelman

God's Love

God's love is everlasting,
Telling of His grace,
Pouring out His mercies
In every clime and place.
Around the world it reaches,
In glorious display,
Precious tidings, hope and majesty,
Making glad the day.

Norma Woodbridge

I Only Had a Moment

I only had a moment
To think of Him today
Some days are far too busy
To even stop to pray.

I only had a moment
To remember what He gave
Through the rushing traffic
Of the world that He had saved.

I only had a moment
To speak to Him in prayer
Or thank Him for His gift to me
In knowing that He cares.

I only had a moment
To spare for Him tonight
Or remember how He died
To give me Eternal Life.

Teresa Gilland

*You observe Him with each
new day and try Him at
every moment!*
Job 7:18

A Garden Is a Holy Place

A garden is a holy place
For springtime from the sod,
Are plants for every season
Wrought by the hands of God.
Fair daffodils and poppies,
No mortals fashioned these
Or placed a choir of songbirds
In budding springtime trees.
Tall hollyhocks and roses
That grace a Summer day,
No mortal can take credit
For sending them my way.

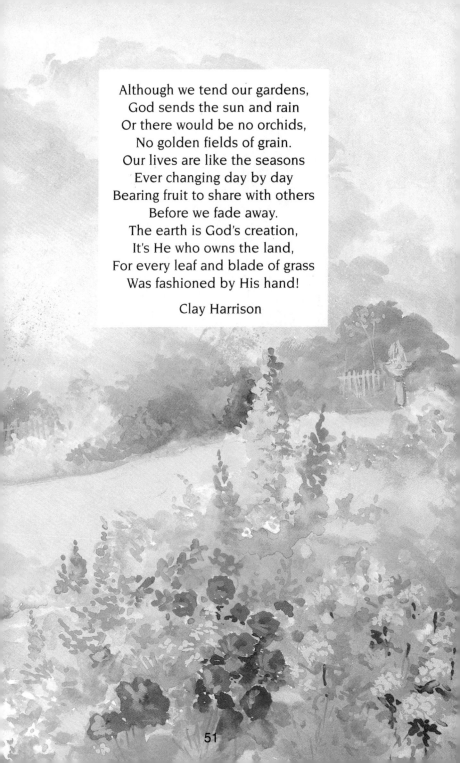

Although we tend our gardens,
God sends the sun and rain
Or there would be no orchids,
No golden fields of grain.
Our lives are like the seasons
Ever changing day by day
Bearing fruit to share with others
Before we fade away.
The earth is God's creation,
It's He who owns the land,
For every leaf and blade of grass
Was fashioned by His hand!

Clay Harrison

Feel the Wonder

Turn your face to the wind
And smell the nectar of Spring,
Embrace the new births
And the freshness they bring.
Look up to budding trees
And see the many new shoots,
Know that they await
The feast of hungry roots.
Lift your eyes to the sky
And feel the warming sun,
Engulf all the grandeur
Three seasons give to one.
Give thanks to our Maker
For it is His work of art,
Everything that He made
Will play a little part.

M. Rosser Lunsford

Friends

Friends are the roses in life's bouquet
Filling our hearts with joy each day,
And when trials and troubles come our way
They bring us comfort as we pray.

Friends are the daffodils, bright yellow tones,
They leave happy thoughts when we are alone;
They bring us laughter and cheer us on
Changing our sadness into happy song.

Friends are the lilacs fragrant and sweet
A gift from God to make life complete.
He knew we'd need someone by our side
To share His love, as in Him we abide.

Roses and lilacs and daffodils,
They help to weather life's troubles and ills.
A friend can laugh or can cry with you –
Thank God for a friend that's kind and true.

Helen Gleason

*For I long to see you, that I
may share with you some
spiritual gift so that you
may be strengthened,*
Romans 1:11

I Want You, Lord

I want to be with You, Lord,
As I begin my day,
To have You as my companion
As I go on my way.

I want to be with You, Lord,
In my thoughts, words and deeds,
To have You as my friend
In meeting all my needs.

I want to be with You, Lord,
To laugh, to cry, to share,
To have you as my partner,
Showing me that you care.

I want to be with You, Lord,
To share my life with You,
To have You as my teacher,
In everything I do.

Please come along with me, Lord;
I want You in my life,
We'll walk the path together,
In good times and in strife.

You promised you'd be here, Lord,
I know that you will be,
We'll always have each other,
Because of You, I'm free.

Bonnie Jones Hardee

Let Your love come to me,
Lord, salvation in accord
with Your promise.
Psalm 119:41

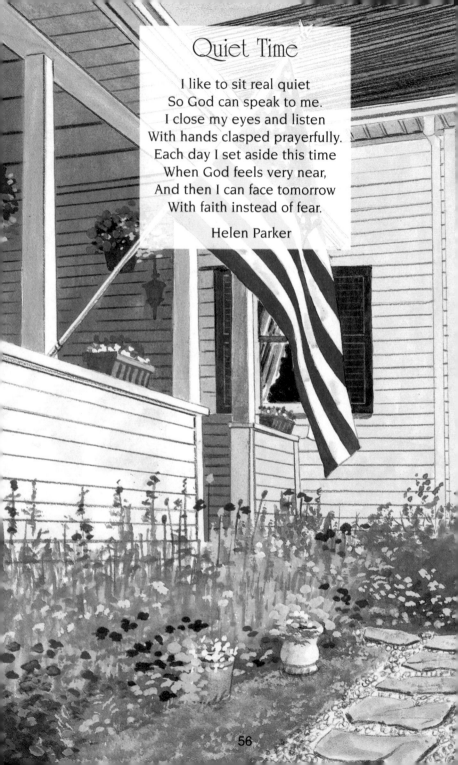

Quiet Time

I like to sit real quiet
So God can speak to me.
I close my eyes and listen
With hands clasped prayerfully.
Each day I set aside this time
When God feels very near,
And then I can face tomorrow
With faith instead of fear.

Helen Parker

Glory Road

I'm on the road to glory
And my Savior waiting there,
Waiting to welcome me home
And take my every care.

My Savior knows I'm coming
And He made a place for me,
A place where there's no sorrow,
With Him in eternity.

I'll be so glad to see Him,
Friends and loved ones too.
We'll all be there in glory
Where He's made all things new.

Dona M. Maroney

*Show Yourself over the heavens,
God; may Your glory appear
above all the earth.
Psalm 57:6*

I See God

I see God's smile in the eyes of a child,
So pure and loving, devoid of guile.
As I offer food to the hungry, I'm blessed,
In their eyes His pleasure and love expressed.
I see Him in loved ones' smiles each day,
He's there when I lift my arms to pray.
In the bonds of friendship, He can be seen,
As upon each other we can lean.
I stand in awe at the beauty around,
The colors of flowers, a bird's sweet sound.
In the soft Summer breeze, the fragrant air,
His wonders are placed for us everywhere.

In warm sunshine He provides for us,
I see His love, and the more I can trust
That there is a Heaven in some high place
That He's allowing us here a taste.
These constant reminders prove to me
All Nature's wonders, on land and sea,
Are prepared by His love for us to see
To show us in part what Heaven will be.
How can we forget one as loving as the Lord?
He also promises us a heavenly reward –
If we will just trust, believe, and obey
We'll share His Heaven some glorious day.

Helen Gleason

Sunshine of a Smile

Smiles are just like sunshine,
Sent from up above.
Smiles are so contagious,
Stirring peace and love.
Smiles will make us happy,
With pride and joy and wealth,
Love God, our heavenly Father,
And neighbors as ourself.
Precious smiles of children
Will brighten up our day –
Such beautiful reminders
To thank the Lord, and pray.
We appreciate all smiles.
Our blessings we will share.
Smiles will have great power
Binding people everywhere.

Edna Massimilla

Then the Lord looked upon the earth,
and filled it with His blessings.
Sirach 16:27

A Guiding Spirit

As we face our fears and troubles
Needless worries linger still…
God has promised us a Savior,
He sees us through and always will.

Do not go through life with worries –
Lift them to the Lord above…
He will bless you and He'll keep you
Safe within his peace and love.

Everyday and everywhere
Our heavenly Father understands…
Never will we walk in darkness,
His Spirit holds us in His hands.

Lift your heart and soul to Jesus –
He gave His life for our sins
Bow before His Holy Spirit…
Faith and hope will live within.

Milly Patzer

A Little Bit of Heaven

There's a little bit of Heaven
In each day that comes anew.
If we truly look we'll find it,
Right there within our view.
The soft, pink mist of early dawn
That tints the morning sky,
A robin in a treetop singing
Praise to God on high.
Bright-eyed children playing near,
A baby's dimpled smile –
A little bit of Heaven sent
To make our day worthwhile.
Rich harvest gifts from Autumn's yield,
Sunsets of red and gold,
Snowflakes gently drifting down
As the Winter days unfold.

Sometimes a bit of Heaven's found
In kindly folks we meet.
If we truly are perceptive,
Rich blessings we will reap.
The friendly smile that warms the heart
When we are feeling down,
Caring people helping others
Wherever need is found.
There's a little bit of Heaven
That comes each day anew.
If we'll take the time to look,
It's right there within our view.

Kay Hoffman

Friendship

Friendship is God's most precious gift;
It enlightens our hearts and minds.
It brings to us true happiness
As love and joy we find.
Treasure greatly, this precious gift
For it remains with us through time.
Material treasures soon disappear
But friendship will remain behind.

Shirley Hile Powell

The Peaceful Kingdom

Lift up your eyes that you may see
Reflections of promised eternity.

Let hope and faith be a guide each day
And live in a kind, loving, joyous way.

Make life a pattern of hope and grace
To meet with our Master face to face.

The gleaming Holy City, ablaze with radiance rare.
Welcomes you to enter and climb the Golden Stair.

Heaven's gates swing open, gold arches sweeping wide,
In God's Peaceful Kingdom, with His glory, you'll abide.

Elisabeth Weaver Winstead

My people will live in
peaceful country, in
secure dwellings and
quiet resting places.
Isaiah 32:18

A Special Friend

Thank you, friend, for bringing
Sunshine to my day.
You seem to have the special knack
Of chasing clouds away.

Perhaps, it is your warm, bright smile,
The thoughtful things you do,
Without pretense or shame,
A friend who's kind and true.

"Come share a cup of tea," You said –
My heart had been so downcast,
You'll never know how much it meant,
Our friendly little chat.

No need to guard my tongue with you
Nor measure what I say,
I know that you will sift my words
In your own kind way.

Thank you, friend, for all the times
You've turned my sky to blue;
I only wish all folk could have
A special friend like you.

Kay Hoffman

Search me, O God, and know my heart; test me and know my anxious thoughts. See if there is any offensive way in me, and lead me in the way everlasting.
Psalm 139:23,24

Help Me Search

Help me search my heart, O God,
To see if there might be
Any unclean thing within
That hinders love in me.
Help me God to conquer fear –
To trust when I question why;
To release the selfish pride I hold
And know that I must try...
To find the best in everyone
Though different we may be,
And show all mankind Your love –
The love you give to me.

Sharon Fuqua

*May all who seek You rejoice and
be glad in You. May those who
long for Your help always say,
"The Lord be glorified."*
Psalm 40:17

My Little Corner of the World

Here I find peace and happiness
Amidst the things I love.
A home alive with mem'ries adds
To blessings from above.

Here I begin each dawning day
With new hope in my heart.
I listen to the song birds sing
And watch the swallows dart.

Sometimes I wander down the path
That leads through meadows green.
The ever babbling, winding brook
Completes the peaceful scene.

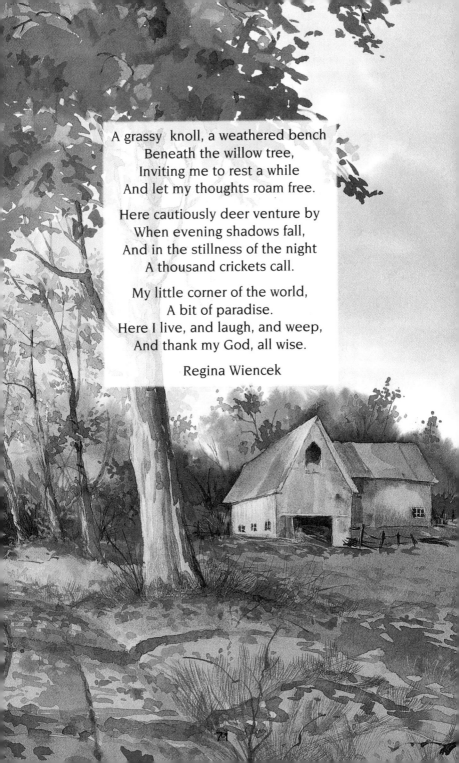

A grassy knoll, a weathered bench
Beneath the willow tree,
Inviting me to rest a while
And let my thoughts roam free.

Here cautiously deer venture by
When evening shadows fall,
And in the stillness of the night
A thousand crickets call.

My little corner of the world,
A bit of paradise.
Here I live, and laugh, and weep,
And thank my God, all wise.

Regina Wiencek

Forever After Friend

You are my forever after Friend,
Dear Lord, because Your love will never die,
I do not have to worry You will tire
Of me and all my problems, by and by.
It doesn't matter if I'm young or old,
Whatever be the color of my hair,
For I have learned to take You at Your word,
Knowing when I call that You will hear.

You will not love me only for awhile,
Then one day roughly cast me to the side,
For Yours is not a human kind of love,
But one for which You suffered and You died.
I am filled with wonder when I think,
To what a vast and infinite degree,
What endless lengths Almighty God would go
... For the love of me.

Grace E. Easley

Angels of the Lord, bless the
Lord, praise and exalt Him
above all forever.
Daniel 3:58

God's Tomorrow

Sometimes there are no answers,
As we trod life's daily way,
For mountains loom ahead of us,
And clouds block the sunshine's ray,
Through it all the beauty of the sun,
Will always shine so bright.
And the lovely golden moonbeams,
Will light the darkest night,
God's hand will touch us lightly,
To steady us, to make us strong,
For His strength will always be there,
At dawn, and through the hours long.
He will bless us and sustain us,
Give us peace and faith each day,
Renew our hope for each tomorrow,
In our lives, His love will stay.

Berniece G. Piercy

A clean heart create for me, God;
renew in me a steadfast spirit.
Psalm 51:12

How Great My God

Oh, how great is this God of mine
Who is loving, merciful, and kind.
This One who guards my very soul
Allows His love and joy to flow.

He always guards me day and night
And keeps me in His precious sight.
He gently pulls me back His way
If perhaps I should happen to stay.

How mighty is my Master's power
As He watches over me every hour.
He has given to me the gift of hope
And grants me the strength to cope.

I know that my God cares for me
And wants me with Him for eternity.
There I'll remain in perfect peace
Where all of my earthly woes will cease.

All things are made by the Creator's hand.
He spreads His beauty across the land.
May the winds of Heaven sing their song
In that glorious place where there is no wrong.

Shirley Hile Powell

Not About Me

It's not about me, it's all about Him,
My God who loves me so.
I never have to fear or doubt
He's with me wherever I go.

His love is everlasting,
It never goes away.
No matter what I say or do,
His love is here to stay.

We must never forget the sacrifice
He made for you and me.
He gave His very own life
To give us eternity.

Is it any wonder
That all my love I give,
I'll worship and honor Him
As long as I shall live.

Dona M. Maroney

Secure in God's Arms

We go about our daily lives
Unencumbered and carefree,
No thoughts of what lies just beyond
On paths for you and me.

But God was there and heard my cry
Whenever I called His name;
He gave me back the breath of life
And eased my frantic pain.

He wrapped me in His loving arms
And made me free, secure.
Oh, how I praise God's holy name;
May my faith in Him endure!

Mary S. Chevalier

*God alone is my rock and
my salvation, my secure
height; I shall not fall.
Psalm 62:7*

Come to Me

Draw me close to You, my God
Let my spirit know,
That You dwell here, inside of me,
Never to let go.
Let me feel Your presence, Lord
As I stumble and I fail,
For only through Your awesome strength
Can my tired soul prevail.
Speak to me, my mighty King,
Through the canyons of my mind,
Inspire me with Your daily love
To be merciful and kind.

Hold my hand, oh Father, God,
As these mountains I must scale,
Provide the endurance that I need
To reach the end of my long trail.
Touch me with Your spirit, Lord,
As You provide all that I need,
And most of all, reveal in me
Your love through every deed.

Carol Lee Grainger

Sweet Relief!

Place your hand in our Father's
When surrounded by the darkness of night,
Let His spirit lead boldly onward
Into the glorious light!
There's strength to remove a mountain,
Faith to believe God can,
Persistence to conquer the obstacles,
Love for our fellowman;
Peace to calm a troubled sea,
Comfort amid the grief,
Joy when sorrows linger,
Patience, hope, sweet relief!

Linda C. Grazulis

Look for the Rainbow

There is not a life without sorrow
Nor is there a heart without pain;
Though dark clouds veil your tomorrow
The sun will come through again.

Today you may feel blue and forsaken,
Wipe away the tears from your eyes.
Another dawn will be breaking
And birds sing beneath cloudless skies.

Today may hold reasons for sighing,
But tomorrow you'll smile again.
Cheer up and look for God's token,
The rainbow after the rain.

Regina Wiencek

*At dawn let me hear of Your kindness, for
in you I trust. Show me the path I should
walk, for to You I entrust my life.*
Psalm 143:8

A Letter to My Lord

How often I have called on You
In my sorrow and my pain,
That you would answer all my prayers
To restore me once again.

I depend on You and trust You
As I come to You this day,
To give me strength and courage
To uplift and guide my way.

My faith has never faltered;
I exhalt and give you praise.
For You, dear Lord, have never failed;
You bring light to my dark days.

I accept your wise decisions
As I wait so patiently,
Knowing that Your love prevails,
That You have always answered me.

I find the calm and peace I need;
My faith in You is multiplied.
I thank You Lord for being there –
All my needs are satisfied.

Patience Allison Hartbauer

But You, Lord, are a shield
around me; my glory, You
keep my head high.
Psalm 3:4

With Warmest Memories

When I was just a little child
I first became aware,
How Jesus loves all His children
And keeps them in His care.

And I remember home so well
Where it was often said,
We kindly thank You, Father
For our food and daily bread.

There was a book with pages worn,
That sat on a table near,
Beside a warm and cozy fire
There was a faded chair.

As I recall my childhood days
It seems that I can see,
A picture clear within my heart
With warmest memories.

Katherine Smith Matheney

*Then He took the bread, said the blessing,
broke it, and gave it to them, saying,
"This is My body, which will be given for
you; do this in memory of Me."*
Luke 22:19

Come to the Garden

Come to the garden
For God is right there.
Each little flower
Is nurtured with care.

God, the Creator
Has each flower planned.
It starts with a seed
By His mighty Hand.

The color – the fragrance –
Each season of year.
In timely conformance
The flowers appear.

So, come to the garden.
And feast on God's power.
For God is right there
In each lovely flower.

Edna Massimilla

*Now then, let the power
of my Lord be displayed
in its greatness.*
Numbers 14:17

To Bless Humanity

Springtime whispers all around
When Nature makes its call,
Arrested from the chill of wind
When leaves began to fall.
Soft light begins to filter through
The pewter skies overhead;
Robins sing and birds on wing
Give praise, it's often said.

God's touch is in each flower's bud,
Each leaf that starts to grow.
He's in the miracle of birth;
The seeds that farmers sow.
He holds life's beauty in His hands
And through His majesty,
Sets forth renewal of all life
To bless humanity.

Nancy Watson Dodrill

Look up to the skies
and behold; regard the
heavens high above you.
Job 35:5

88

God's Garden

I often walk in God's garden
Beneath pale azure skies,
Amongst the trees and flowers
And brightly colored butterflies.
Roses bright with color,
Beautifully shaped blooms,
Fill the air with fragrance –
Sweet smelling perfume.
Carpets of golden daffodils,
Dainty petals slowly unfold.
Beauty from each fragile flower –
Such pleasure to behold.
Carried by gentle breezes
Sweet warbling notes
Of joyful birds' musical sounds –
Upon the air, they float.
God in all His graciousness
Lends His garden to you and I,
The people of His world,
Beneath His wondrous sky.

Jacqui Richardson

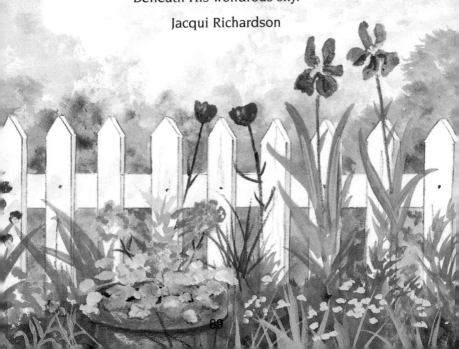

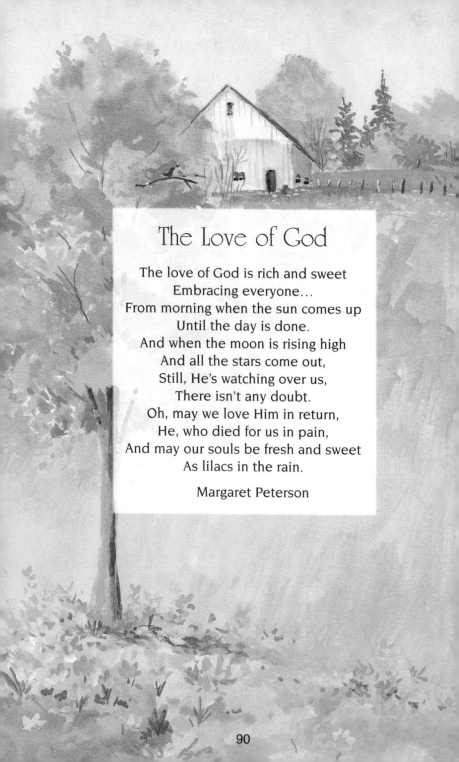

The Love of God

The love of God is rich and sweet
Embracing everyone…
From morning when the sun comes up
Until the day is done.
And when the moon is rising high
And all the stars come out,
Still, He's watching over us,
There isn't any doubt.
Oh, may we love Him in return,
He, who died for us in pain,
And may our souls be fresh and sweet
As lilacs in the rain.

Margaret Peterson

The Artist in My Yard

The red of a cardinal,
The blue of a jay,
Gold finch with their yellow;
All coming my way.
The green of a warbler,
The gray of a dove;
Beautiful colors
From an artist, with love.
The blue of the skies,
The green of the trees,
Bright yellow butterflies
Dance in the breeze.
A puffy white cloud
With pale shades of pink;
A palette of colors,
I pause and I think.
Who is this artist
Who paints in my yard?
I know it's my friend,
My Savior, my Lord!

Mary Ann Houston

*God knows the way to
it; it is He who is
familiar with its place.*
Job 28:23

Shared Joys

I like to share with you, my friend,
The beauties of this day.
The golden sun, the cloudless sky,
Bright flowers on display.
Through shady lanes I like to stroll
With you close by my side,
To share the happiness within,
The joy I cannot hide.

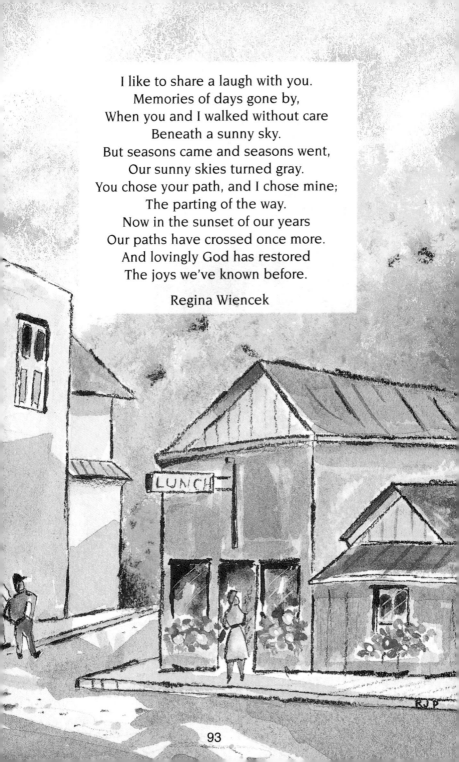

I like to share a laugh with you.
Memories of days gone by,
When you and I walked without care
Beneath a sunny sky.
But seasons came and seasons went,
Our sunny skies turned gray.
You chose your path, and I chose mine;
The parting of the way.
Now in the sunset of our years
Our paths have crossed once more.
And lovingly God has restored
The joys we've known before.

Regina Wiencek

I See the Lord

In flaming sunset glow,
In moonlight on the snow,
Dashing waves upon the shore,
I see the Lord and I adore!

On purple mountains high,
In rainbows in the sky,
Flowers around my door,
I see the Lord and I adore!

In little birds that fly,
And bunnies all so shy,
Kittens on the floor,
I see the Lord and I adore!

In pine trees, oh so tall,
Where rain drops softly fall,
Where mighty eagles soar,
I see the Lord and I adore!

Bernice Laux

Trees

Rustling leaves – a sighing breeze
Gently whispers in the trees,
Precious moments in the rain
As the leaves turn green again,
Birds are nesting in the Spring
Lending songs they fondly sing.
I am sure all trees have known
A lovely language all their own,
Reaching upward to the sky
Touched by beauty there on high,
Just before the break of day
Hiding dark of night away.
Come and sit awhile today,
'Neath my branches where children play;
Cooling moments – happy fun
Shelter from the blazing sun,
Enjoy the gentle Summer breeze
'Neath God's lovely spreading trees.

Garnett Ann Schultz

Every perfect gift is from above,
coming down from the Father of
lights with whom there is no
variation or shifting shadow.

James 1:17

God's Perfect Gifts

God knows the perfect time to give us gifts
That cheer the heart and soothe our aching pain.
He knows the perfect way to love and lift
Our spirits so that we can laugh again.

His gifts may come in many different forms;
A butterfly upon a newborn rose…
A rainbow showing we can weather storms…
A sunset softly drawing to a close.

Sometimes He sends His gifts through other's hands;
A loving word from someone kind and dear…
A smile that shows a good friend understands…
A hug that comforts, helps us persevere.

God wraps His gifts in most unusual ways;
When we untie them sunlight fills our days.

Claire Ottenstein-Ross

Lord, You are kind and
forgiving, most loving to
all who call on You.
Psalm 86:5

Find your delight in the Lord who will give you your heart's desire.
Psalm 37:4

A Friend Is a Friend...

Friends are refreshing as showers
On a sultry Summer day,
As welcome as glorious sunshine
On a dark and dreary way;
As sweet as the fragrance of roses
Still wet with sparkling dew;
Delightful as morning praises
Of birds, when the day is new;
Gentle as evening breezes
Cooling the weary brow,
Embracing you with compassion,
Lifting your burdens, somehow.
A friend is a friend in all seasons,
When mirth and laughter ring.
A friend is a friend in sorrow
When the heart is too heavy to sing.
A friend is a friend in the good times
When good fortune smiles on you,
But let the winds of adversity blow:
A friend remains faithful and true.

Regina Wiencek

Quiet Time With God

Hush, my dear child,
And listen to my voice.
I will speak of a love
That will make you rejoice.
The love that I offer
Man cannot comprehend,
Nor the gifts of the Father
That He deems to send.
Rise above the bustle
Of your busy daily life,
And give Me your sorrows,
Troubles, pains, and strifes.
Grant Me some quiet time
And speak to Me when you pray,
Then we will remain together
Throughout your busy day.

Shirley Hile Powell

Speak Jesus' Name

Let mouths be not frozen
To tell the Lord,
How His infinite love
To us is outpoured.

Tell how He walks with us
Uphill and down,
Through verdant meadows,
Through cities and towns.

Tell of His mercy,
His longsuffering, too,
Extended to each one,
To me and to you.

Let mouths be not frozen
To speak Jesus' name;
He's God and our Savior,
Forever He'll reign.

Loise Pinkerton Fritz

God Knows

God sees when we're selfish
And think just of self,
When the chance to help others
Is put on the shelf.

He grieves when we falter
And give into sin,
For He knows without question
We're troubled within.

He smiles when we're trying
To follow His lead
To help those who are lonely
And those who are in need.

For God is all-seeing,
Our Father, best friend,
Bestowing His blessings
As on Him we depend.

And as we seek guidance,
Our faith firm and true,
He'll never forsake us,
Whatever we do.

Vi B. Chevalier

At dawn may the Lord bestow
faithful love that I may sing
praise through the night, praise
to the God of my life.
Psalm 42:9

One Sunday Afternoon

It was a Summer's day delight!
All of Nature sang;
Though quiet were the flowers bright,
Their harmonies began.

And I was on a hilltop high,
The sky a placid blue:
The beauty of its soundlessness
Oh! That was music too!

I need not speak of songbirds sweet,
For they were all in tune;
When Nature played her symphony
One Sunday afternoon.

George R. Kossik

*May the God of endurance and
encouragement grant you to think
in harmony with one another, in
keeping with Christ Jesus.*
Romans 15:5

My Mountain Home

The moon is full, the woods are deep,
Below the world is lost in sleep,
The air is crisp, so cool and clear,
Far off the singing stream I hear.

Just God and I together roam
This wilderness, my mountain home,
My soul is born again where He
Does seem so close and dear to me.

The nighthawk sails the starry sky,
The soft wind hums her lullaby,
The black bear and the old raccoon
Must find a den for sleeping soon.

For not too long from now I know
The mountain will be hushed in snow,
A wonderland these hills will be
As far as any man can see.

And I, by God, so very blest
Before the fire will sit and rest,
In warmth and peace I'll have no care
With those I love beside me there!

Kate Watkins Furman

In His Care

Just put your trust in Jesus
And He'll always see you through.
That dreary trial you're facing –
He's waiting there for you.
Reach out for His hand in faith
As you walk that long, dark road.
He'll gladly take your burden
And lighten that heavy load.
Raise your voice and praise Him
For always being there.
Remember how He loves you,
You're ever in His care.

Dona M. Maroney

A Guiding Spirit

As we face our fears and troubles
Needless worries linger still…
God has promised us a Savior;
He sees us through and always will.

Do not go through life with worries;
Lift them to our Lord above.
He will bless you and He'll keep you
Safe within His peace and love.

Everyday and in everyway
Our heavenly Father understands.
Never will we walk in darkness;
His Spirit holds us in His hands.

Lift your heart and soul to Jesus;
He gave His life for our great sin.
Bow before His Holy Spirit…
Faith and Hope will live within.

Milly Patzer

*You are my rock and my
fortress; for Your name's
sake lead and guide me.*
Psalm 31:4

Cast all your worries
upon Him because He
cares for you.
1 Peter 5:7

Country Lane

Give me a road away from the crowd,
Away from the noise and the race
And let me wander the quiet trail
To a different time and place.

Where miles are measured in valleys,
And birches point the way
To somewhere we miss so dearly –
We call it yesterday.

All cares are soon forgotten
On the path of no intent;
The beauty of the countryside
Is surely heavensent.

And when this journey's over
The memories shall remain
Of daydream trips into the past
And down a country lane.

C. David Hay

My people will live in peaceful country, in
secure dwellings and quiet resting places.
Isaiah 32:18

The Three-in-One Divine

We need the Holy Spirit
To guide us through each day
To warn us when in danger,
And lead us on our way.

We need our God almighty
To teach us how to live
Our Savior Jesus, our best friend,
The One who came to give.

Jill Lemming

Sing to God, praise the divine
name; exalt the rider of the clouds.
Rejoice before this God whose
name is the Lord.
Psalm 68:5

The Voice Within

Listen to the voice within
And you will surely find
Directions meant to live by,
And new-found peace of mind.

Listen with your inner ear
And you will surely hear
God's voice and purpose for your life
Unfold and become clear.

Listen with a faithful heart
And you will come to know
God's hand is guiding you and me
With love where're we go...

And as we journey through the years
Undaunted, head held high,
Through tribulations and through tears,
God knows that we have tried.

Vi B. Chevalier

May Peace Like a River...

May peace like a river
Flow through your life
And wash away sorrows
To lessen your strife.
May peace like a river
Bring you pleasant dreams
As you walk through green pastures
By cool mountain streams.
May the spirit within you
Bring comfort today
And bring peace and courage
You need for the day.

May peace like a river
Bring showers of love
And your burdens be lifted
On the wings of a dove.
May angels surround you
By day and by night,
And where there is darkness,
Shed heavenly light.
May God answer your prayers
And banish your strife...
May peace like a river
Flow through your life.

Clay Harrison

My eyes long to see Your promise.
When will You comfort me?
Psalm 119:82

Let Me Be a Blessing, Lord

Let me be a blessing, Lord
To all who pass my way;
Walk with me and guide me
In all I do and say.
Lead me to the lonely ones
That I might bring them cheer;
To show I care and want to help
And that You are always near.
Let me share with others
Your covenant and creed;
Help me to instill new faith
Let me fill their void and need.
I strive to serve You faithfully
To channel hope in Your accord;
Empower me, show me the way
Then let me be a blessing, Lord.

Patience Allison Hartbauer

Peace...

It is a feeling of relief,
Of quiet and of rest;
It often comes when you're alone
And you feel truly blessed...

You feel it when you're with a friend
Of whom you're very fond;
You see it in a starlit sky,
Or on a golden pond...

It happens when you can relax
In some familiar chair;
It fills your heart with happiness,
Just like a precious prayer...

And should there ever come a time,
When you need sweet release,
God's always near to comfort you,
And He will bring you peace!

Hope C. Oberhelman

The Lord look upon you kindly
and give you peace!
Numbers 6:26

Where His Love Abides

Gone are the days of yesteryears
When I walked the path of sin.
I shudder when I realize
What a sinner I had been.

Somewhere in time, my God reached down
And lifted up this unworthy soul;
Up to the realms of happiness,
Far from the world below.

He gazed into my frightened eyes
And smiled lovingly into my face.
God told me He had claimed me,
Then filled me with His grace.

Once filled with His Holy Spirit
My life was no longer my own.
The joy and happiness that we share
Comes from my God alone.

The love that now engulfs me
Is a gift beyond compare.
Everything that He has given me
Was meant for me to share.

Now as I walk the path of life
With my Savior by my side,
My heart is filled with peace at last
For that is where His love abides.

Shirley Hile Powell

*How precious is Your love,
O God! We take refuge in
the shadow of Your wings.*
Psalm 36:8

In the Valley

When we are lost and wondering
And seeking for His love,
We only need cry out to Him
And wait for grace above.

The good and faithful Shepherd
Takes us by the hand,
And in the bleak of darkness,
He leads to safer land.

Our heavy hearts hear, "Peace, be still."
We know we're not alone.
From the valley where we wandered,
He leads us now back home.

Ruthmarie Brooks Silver

Mighty God Is He

He is the Lord of the Universe
Of power and of might;
He rules the sun by day
He rules the moon by night.
He rocks the highest mountains
With thundering and roars,
And makes the mighty seas to roll
On the oceans sandy shores.
He knows each thought we're thinking,
Each desire in our heart;
He's concerned with every detail
Of our needs the smallest part.
He creates all Nature's beauty
For all of us to see;
Yet concerned with the smallest sparrow
He feeds it faithfully.
Is this not a God to worship
To fear and to adore,
For on Him depends our destiny
If we would reach Heaven's shore.

Helen Gleason

Arise, Lord, in Your power!
We will sing and chant the
praise of Your might.
Psalm 21:14

The Promise

Nature holds the promise of
Eternal things above,
Reflections of our Creator
Who showers us with love.
Nature reinvents herself
As seasons come and go.
The bulbs we plant in Autumn
In Spring begin to grow.
In Spring's a resurrection
When Winter snows depart,
Assurance that life goes on,
Reborn in every heart.

We feast our eyes on beauty
Wherever we may go,
For Nature provides memories
That set our hearts aglow.
When Winter comes we oft forget
The blessings we behold,
Blinded by the falling snow,
Chilled by the numbing cold.
When Nature brings us to our knees,
She shows us God is love.
Nature holds the promise of
Eternal things above.

Clay Harrison

At Times Like These...

How precious the words "I love you,"
When the day is trying and gray,
When your little world is falling apart,
And you are too weary to pray.
How fitting a word of assurance
From the lips that whisper "I care."
How gentle the arms that embrace you
When your burdens are heavy to bear.
How welcome a shoulder to lean on
When you lack the strength to go on.
How precious the words "I love you"
To a heart that has lost its song.

Regina Wiencek

I Thank God for You

How blessed I've been throughout my life,
So many happy days I've known,
Because you are a part of them
With all the loving care you've shown.
I know that God arranged for me
To have you share my days;
You give me strength, you uplift me
In so many countless ways.
Your love, assurance, faithfulness
Help to make me strong;
My life is filled with sunshine
My heart is filled with song.
I smile in sweet contentment
At all the thoughtful things you do.
Yes, I am blessed and I rejoice
As I am thanking God for you.

Patience Allison Hartbauer

The Searching

I searched the wide world over;
I looked both far and near
In my eager quest for my heart to be blest
And be free of its doubt and fear.
I searched throughout the countryside;
I roamed all around the city
But found nothing there that would compare
To the joy that's awaiting me!
For soon in a nighttime vision
There at the foot of my bed,
I found what I long had searched for
And this is what He said…

"Arise, My child from your weariness,"
And with His outstretched arms,
He cradled me there with His tender care
And shielded me from all harm.
Now I walk with my Savior, hand in hand,
And gone are the struggles and strife.
He taught me to see and understand
He's the way, the truth and the life.

Lou Ella Cullipher

Make me understand the way
of Your precepts; I will ponder
Your wondrous deeds.
Psalm 119:27

Our Forgiving Heavenly Father

I am so blessed to be God's child,
He's done so much for me;
He sent His only, precious Son
My sinful soul to free.

To name my blessings, one by one,
Would be an arduous task –
But I have found for all my needs,
Through prayer, I merely ask.

What Friend is there when trials come
On whom I can always depend?
Who would do such wondrous things,
Watch o'er me without end?

Only the Father in Heaven's fair land
Could impart such absolute love,
Could forgive my sins of faithlessness,
Then receive me in that home above!

Mary S. Chevalier